© David Philip Publishers 2018

© Text & Illustrations 2018 Thembinkosi Kohli

First published in 2018 by
David Philip Publishers, 6 Spin Street, Cape Town 8001

All rights reserved. No part of this publication may be produced, stored in or introduced into a retrieval system, or transmitted, in any form or by any means (electronic, mechanical, photocopying, recording or otherwise), without the prior written permission of the publisher. Any person who does any unauthorised act in relation to this publication may be liable to criminal prosecution and civil claims for damages.

ISBN: 978-1-4856-2683-1
E pub ISBN: 978-1-4856-2742-5
E mobi ISBN: 978-1-4856-2753-1

Typesetting: Hybrid Creative
Printed and bound in the Republic of South Africa by Novus Print Solutions.

David Philip is committed to a sustainable future for our business, our readers and our planet.

Wake up! Wake up!

Turn off the tap!

We drink water.

Water washes my toy car.

Do not throw rubbish into water.

We swim in clean water.

Fish live in water.

Fish keep us alive.

Water helps the sunflower grow.

Water helps the tree grow.

I am a star.

I touch the clouds.

I collect water from the clouds.

Clean water helps us live.

Please turn off the taps and save water.

We are water,
and water is us.